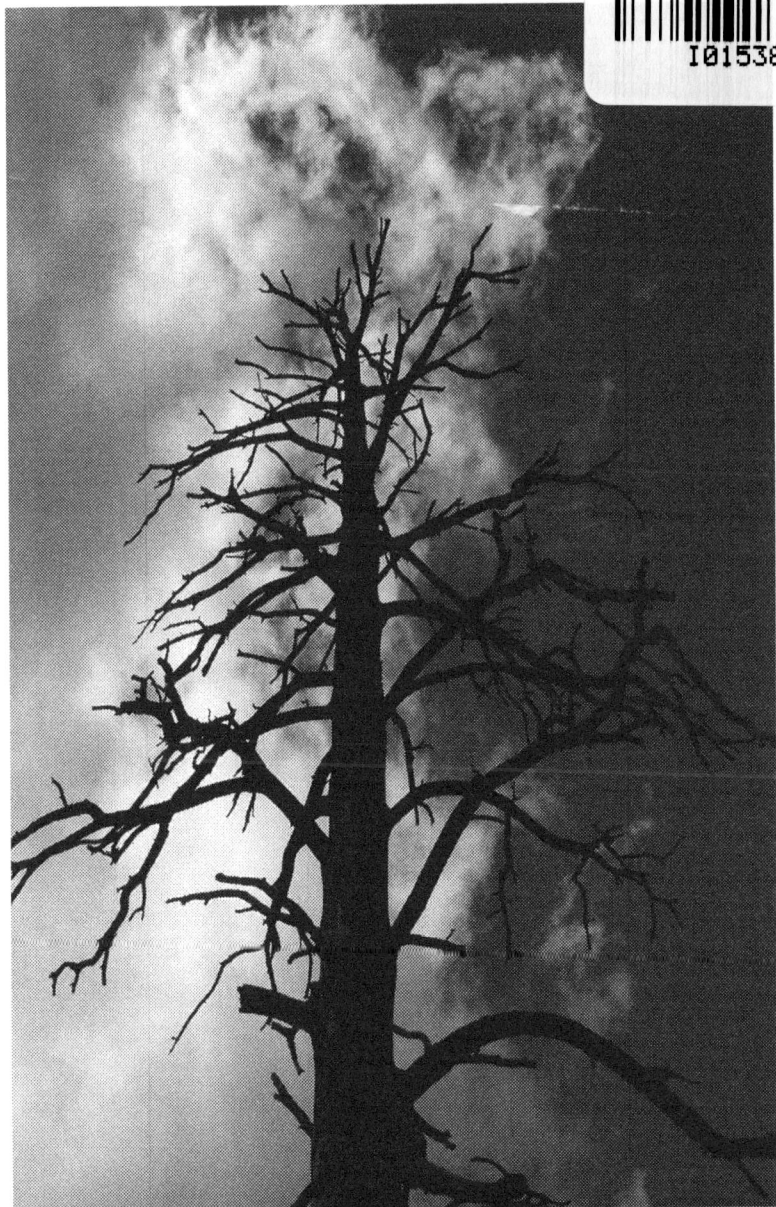

A Blaze of Light

a book of poems

by Molly Brogan

A Blaze of Light

A Book of Poems

By Molly Brogan

ALSO BY Molly Brogan

A Blaze of Light Published By Molly Brogan Enterprises

Copyright © 2007 by Molly Brogan

ISBN 978 0 6151 4236 4

Cover photograph by Gerald Klida

Cover Design By Molly Brogan Enterprises

Illustrations by Gerald Klida, Robert Parker, Edward Brogan

Printed in the United States of America

For Information:

Molly Brogan Enterprises

mbrogan@mc.net

D EDICATION

This book is dedicated to my beloved husband, Gerald Klida, through whom all things are possible.

TABLE OF CONTENTS

Remember Me

Chasing Twilight

Remember Me
by Molly Brogan

Remember Me

Remember me
Near the long day's end
When moonlight
Initiates your heart
To the journey of your soul.

Remember me clearly
As I stand, paused,
Listening for your soft entreat,
Waiting to offer a touch of kindness,
Understanding what you have to offer,
Your mind, emotion and being.

As our spirits fly
In parting dance
I will wrap you in comfort
And keep you close
Until you next
Remember me.

Chasing Twilight

by Molly Brogan

Hello

You are
So familiar to me.
As we reveal
Our stories
To each other
Your words
Your phrasing
Your rhythms
Your images
Are all so familiar.

They create a stirring inside
That compels me
To keep reaching for you,
Keep writing you.
My curiosity
Grows with every letter.
Excitement fills
Each morning and evening
As I rediscover myself
While writing to you.

Your words
Tell your story
And explain your character
And touch me
In ways I can't explain.
And I now look forward
To each and every day.
Look forward to taking you
Farther inside me
So that I can know
And remember
Who you are.
And who I am.

Discovery

Beyond the excitement
And the flirtation
And the rhetoric
There is a hint
Of something soulful.
Something as familiar
As a mother's touch
Or coming home
Or a favorite song.

The problem with hints
Is that we aren't sure:
How much of what we see
Actually comes
From desire and hope
And how much
Is really there
Waiting
Like an unopened gift
On a coming-of-age
Birthday.

We won't know for sure
Until the opening
The revelation
The moment of discovery
Until then
We set our course
To that destination
By touching
With words
Thoughts
And desires.

Until then
We wait breathlessly
Cultivating hope
With prayer
Making ready
Ourselves
And our lives
For the time

When we can
Receive eachother
And give eachother
Everything saved
For the moment
When our two souls
Meet again
And remember
The sacred place
We always share.

Beginning

I feel a beginning
Within me
And all around me,
Like I am
Opening forward,
And you are
Wrapped around me
Like the soft
Summer air.

I find you
Each night
In one dream
After another,
Always so welcoming.
Taking me into you
On the beach,
In the water,
In a cloud
Of desire,
Or a field
Of soft fresh flowers.
You always find me
And hold me
Until the next dream,
Until the next promise.

And so I wake
Each morning
With you
All over me
And a big smile
To greet the day.
It becomes so easy
To take on
The day's problems,
Knowing that in-between
You will be there
In word
And spirit
And invitation

Of the next encounter
Tomorrow
And yesterday,
Forever
In each moment
With you.

Promise

I see in you
Such promise
And possibility.
I feel in you
Excitement,
Hope,
And earnest desire
To come closer,
To explore together
This life,
Each other.

You suggest
We travel.
Place ourselves
In foreign surroundings
So that our adventure
Together
Can be
Inside/outside,
Complete.

You suggest
We search our souls
And choose
A place
Familiar
Yet unexplored
In this life.

A fabulous idea.
We can then unfold
On all levels
Simultaneously
From depth to detail,
Moment to eternity.

Is this by design,
Or by instinct?
Is it intention
Or natural curiosity

That compels you
To place us
Where the spark
Will instantly
Set our souls ablaze?

I hope
That you can stand
The heat
Of the extreme intimacy
You seek
But have not yet found
In this lifetime.

My answer to you
Is yes, please.
Bring on the heat
With your promise.
I know we
Can create it.
I hope we
Can sustain it.

Forever

When
Did we begin
Our free fall
Into heaven
Into eachother
Into the place
Where our spirits reside
And call to us
Each moment?

It seems just yesterday
Or an eternity
That we said hello
That familiar echo
That instantly brought
Us here again
Together again
Even though
We remain
Miles apart.

Never before
Have I known
Someone
So completely.
Never have I
Felt so deeply.
Not in this life
Did I expect
To fly to such heights
To open so wide
To see so clearly
The possibility of us.

Time becomes
Irrelevant
Because each moment
You are with me
And in me
Filling emotion
To the brim

Changing the future
Changing my viewpoint
Changing awareness
Forever.

Please don't ever leave.
I can't go back.
Can't un-know
What I now know.
It is true,
Two can be one
Now and forever
In each thought
And each moment.
Connection
Can be so clear
So pure
And so strong
That it can last
Forever
And bring forever
To our finite lives
To our days and nights
To our touch
And our words
And our love.

Anticipation

I know
It is impossible
For us
To be
In the same space
Always.

The anticipation
In between
Is amazing.

Sometimes,
When you are gone,
I can actually
Feel you with me.
Your sweet mouth
On my mouth,
Your hand
On the side of my head
Caressing
While we kiss.

My body feels it
As if you are here.
With me,
Loving me,
Always,
In all ways.

You fill me,
My heart,
My soul,
My life.
Like color
Fills a painting
Or words
Fill a poem
Or two
Free spirits
Fill their love.

Touch Me

You touch me in ways
I never thought possible.
I wonder
If you understand
What you do
Or how you do it.
Or is it simply
The natural result
Of your sweet love.

You touch my heart
And open feeling
Of such power
And magnitude
That it washes away
All doubt and fear
Leaving a peace
That seems contagious
To all around me.

You touch my body
And create a passion
That instantly draws
Our world
Into the moment
And this moment
Becomes every moment
And the only moment
Endlessly.

You touch my spirit
And we begin
Our flight
To the realm
Where all is possible
Through our love.
Where we explore
Possibility
With new dimension
Healing each other.
Healing our world.

Expanding our love
Farther into forever.

You touch my soul
And awaken it
To the depths of our
Experience together.
You clarify
Who I am
Who I was
And who I will be
Through your touch.
Through our love,
My love.

Hesitation

You are so inviting
With your warm
Generous greeting
You bring me
Into you
With a rush of excitement
A kaleidoscope of ideas
A blanket of sweet words
That warms my soul
And comforts
Like parent's lap.
When I am
All locked in,
Completely yours,
You hesitate.
And ask me to wait
For the readiness
That you now reveal
Like a new game piece,
A sudden barrier.

So I agree
To wait again for you
While you resume seduction
Into the world of US.
You seem so certain
Of this world
And its possibility.
Until it is time
To make it real.

Then comes
The hesitation.
Is it self doubt?
Insufficient trust?
No room in our life?
No room in your heart?
What keeps our world
In the air, afloat
On our paper ship
That sails the course

Between fantasy
And reality?

And why do you hesitate
To reveal it?
Do you fear
Disagreement?
Harsh reaction?
Disappointment?

Have you forgotten
Who I am
And how I play?

Comes to Light

What happens to me
When I think that I know you,
And unexpectedly find
That I misunderstood
Your signals
And words
And intentions?

Something hidden
Comes to light.
I suddenly see it.
And it readjusts
My entire perception.
My place in the world.
Your place in my heart.

Emotion floods me.
And I pull back.
I observe myself,
And the emotion.
I want to be able to choose it.
Hope that it doesn't choose me.

I struggle to see that
It isn't my only choice.
That at least, I can not choose it.
And not worry
About where that non choice leaves me.
Embrace the nothingness
That may take its place.

Joy, love, happiness
Would be better.
I have become accustom
To those emotions.
Resting in your arms.
Secure in your love.
Until something hidden
Comes to light.

Will it take both of us
To sort this out?
Or will I need
To go it alone.
Individually.
I prefer sharing
But am prepared
To make the individual choice.
Without emotion.
Unless, that is what I choose.

Can You

There are times
When you
Are hard to hold
In the place
Where our spirits meet
And love.
Times when we
Cannot be together
There.

Something or other
Obstructs
The flow of us.
Halts the dance
We dance inside.
Dims the connection
Needed to know us
Without physical touch.

What are those things
That keep us from eachother?
That provides resistance
To our love's current
That flows endlessly
Into forever?
Can we find them?
Reduce them?
Eliminate them?
Prevent them?

You accept them
As life's burden
And seem
Unwilling to self examine
Or analyze
The process.

Is it because
You cannot
Experience US inside
As I do?

You proclaim
That experience
As your goal
But will not plan
Your objectives
To obtain it.

So I begin to worry.
Do we share
This value
Of spiritual freedom,
Of love
In all
Its glorious depth,
In the flight
Of two as one?
Can you see this
As I do?
Or if not,
Are you willing
To follow my lead
And discover
The true intimacy
Of US together?

Once

Once, for an eternal moment
I could reach for you with my heart
And find you, eagerly waiting
To touch me completely.

Once, and not so long ago
I could think of you
With total love
And you would answer
With a letter, or a phone call
Before the thought had ended.

Once, whenever fear gripped me
Making my need for you
Instant and absolute,
You knew it
And came to me immediately,
Before I could ask.

Once, you responded
To each of my entreats
Tenderly, entirely
So that our dance of passion
Traversed depths before unimagined
And since untouched.

Now, we are locked in five senses
Living like others do
Without those rare qualities
Of souls linked
And spirits in constant communion.

Here, I will revel in those five senses
Taking my fill of them every moment
Learning all I can of you through them,
The sweetness, the light,
The focal connection they provide
To awareness, as occasionally
They combine and blow the lid
From sensory constraints
That define us.

And our souls connect and open
Without needing the rest.

Because wherever you are
Is extreme sweetness for me
When I am there also.

Slipping Away

As sure as I felt
The affinity
And the attraction
That brought you
Farther into me
Than anyone
Has ever been,
I now feel
You slipping away.

Just as I could
Do nothing to stop
My free-fall into love,
It seems
I cannot stop you
From walking away.

What I cannot fathom
Is why.
But know
That is
The taboo question,
The place
Between us
That you will not
Acknowledge.

I do what I can
To hold on
To what remains,
And stop
My breaking heart
From crying out
To your deaf ears,
And drive you
Further into hiding.

But how can I stop
My heart from howling
For what could be,
And what was

So many times
Between us?

You know
It is real
In our hearts
And our spirits,
Yet walk away
From our lives
Together,
While I shake
My head
In disbelief.
I only hope
That disbelief
And heartbreak
Does not make me
An unbeliever
In love
Forever.

Fill the Void

I have already begun
To fill the void
Left when you withdrew your love.

Other spirits
Have replaced yours
While I meditate.
Spirits that show me ways
To substitute the love making
With other quests
In places where our spirits met.

Dreams of healing
Have replaced the erotic dreams
That we once shared.
They heal while rebuilding brick by brick
Areas of the soul washed out
By the flash flood of our desire.

Books have filled the hours
That we spent talking.
Sharing our beings
Exchanging emotion,
Expanding ourselves,
Nourishing our love.

Sleeping pills
Keep me sleeping
So that I do not watch
The hours tick by
While the phone does not ring.
There is no other way
To fill the infinite emptiness left
With the end of nightly pillow talk.

Quiet has replaced that silly laugh
That came and went
With the rush of our passion.
The laugh that expressed joy
And the excitement of deep abiding love
Found unexpectedly like a buried treasure.

A serious face
Replaces the goofy smile
That brought joy
To everyone around me.
A quiet, wry smile
Is now all
I can occasionally muster.

I will welcome
Forgetfulness
When its blessings
Cover me in comfort
And carry me on.
I pray each moment
That it comes very soon
To take away my pain.

Love's Alchemy

Where do I begin
To turn down the fire
To remove the necessity
To let go of the need
In the love I feel for you?

I have never before
Tried so hard
To turn such passionate love,
Into the love of friendship.
A friendship that will last,
Because I don't want
To lose you forever,
But know
That you no longer have room
In your life
For my complete love.

There must be a way
To stop my mind
From turning to you
To stop the emotion
Before it sweeps me away
Into desire
And soulful yearning.
I am determined, love
To find that way.

I check each response
Before I offer it to you.
Comparing it to one
I would offer a friend
Making sure
It remains
Within those boundaries.

No easy chore,
Because not so long ago
Your love took me to places
Before uncharted.
Into rapture
And dances of the spirit

Where we reveled
In eachother
For such a short time,
But no longer share.

And while so much of me
Wants that back,
I resign myself
To offering only
The love of a friend
Of the inner circle.
One that I can tell
The most private secrets
Of my spirit's journey.

Each time I reach for you
With my heart
And you do not respond
This task becomes easier
My love simmers down.

Each time experience
Calls for sharing
With a partner
Or Soul Mate
And you are not there,
The alchemy ignites
And the transformation
Of our love
Becomes more complete.

Each time you tell me
That the way to me
Is impossible for you,
You make it much easier
For me to accept our fate.
The fate that you defined
By not choosing us.

My hope is
That when my work is done,
And our love has undergone
The necessary alchemy,
And quantum changes

Create our new boundaries,
We will find a way
To remain close friends
Through all of the trials
That life brings.
Because you are still
Essential to me
And always will be.

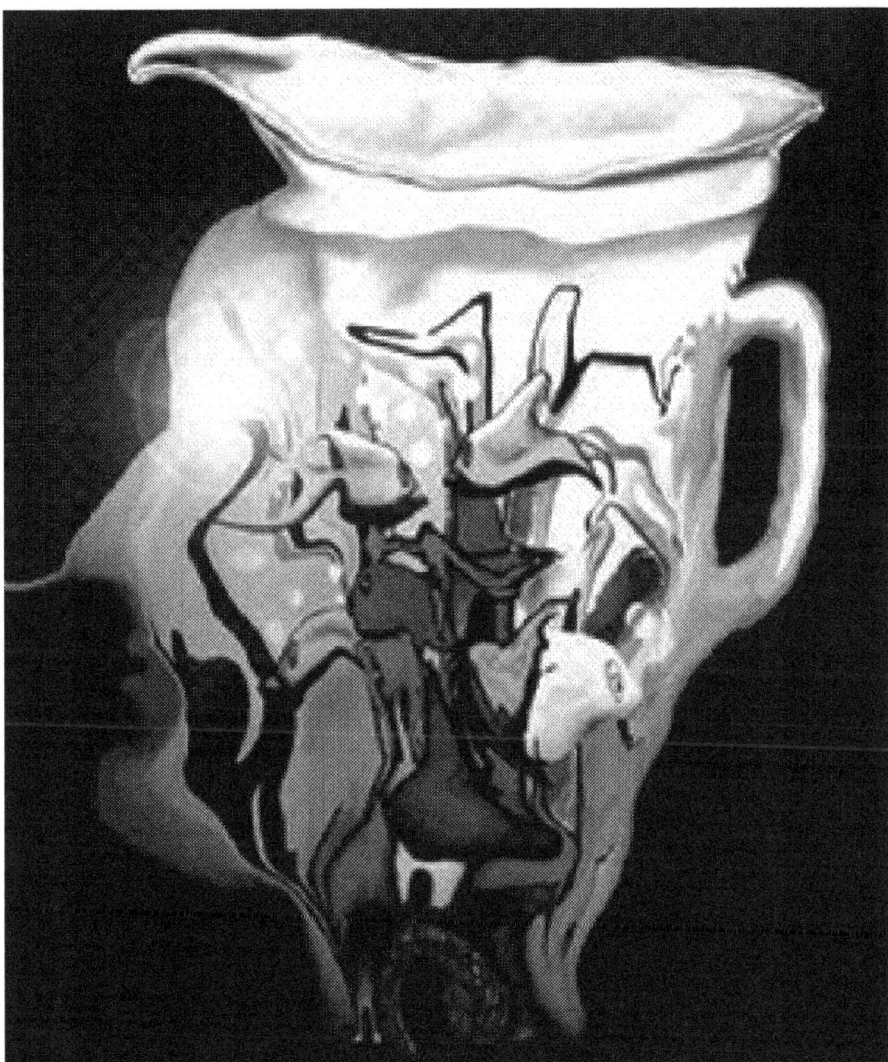

Shadow Dancing

by Molly Brogan

Boundless

How is it
That I can feel you
So close beside me
So strongly
Within me
With every move
Every sigh
Every whisper.

How is it
That I can see you
Blue eyes shining
So clearly
Before me
Your bright smile
Knowing
All of me.

What is it
That awaits us
With the feel
Of something brilliant
Coming
In warm waves
From inside out
And in again.

When is it
That I will begin
To breathe
A natural rhythm
In and out
Instead of this
constant breath
Toward you.

Why is it
That I feel
So boundless
So lost

When I have
Found my life
Again
When I found
you.

For Ever

I swim in the water
That gives birth
To us,
That nourishes
Our desire
To be whole,
To light the way,
To create
The place inside
For others to follow.

I walk
the golden path
Rising from the dead
That leads
To the chalice
I hold for you,
You fill for me,
We allow.

Who will swim
There now
That we are gone,
Moving on
To create the more
To allow
What Is possible
With us?

Who will walk
Our path
Of all and void,
That shines white gold,
That brings
All seasons,
That is
Everywhere?

Will you join me
At the pool's source
Where our eyes meet
Where our dreams begin and end
Where our light shines bright
For ever?

Heart to Heart

Heart to heart
Our connection
Streams through us,
Pulling us through time,
Pulling us together.

We remain
Hearts wide open,
Anticipating,
Accepting.
Feeling hard
With every part
That we call ours.
Feeling softly
With eachother.

We hold eachother here,
In this expanding,
Eternal space.
Here in creation,
We create
Our Usness.

We understand
In retrospect
As we examine
Our recent past,
Our words
And feelings
Given with love.

We understand
In real time
As we intend
Our energy exchange,
In original moments,
That we share
And know
Without words.

We understand
In NOTIME
As we come together
To heal source
To explore
The creative realm
Of the creator
That is ours,
That only we
Were born
To discover
As destiny,
As promise,
As fortune.

We wait
Together,
For what is to come,
Breathless,
Hopeful,
Blessed
With shared vision
And mutual faith.

In Love

Moving now
With love
Farther into light
With you.

Opening now
With possibility
Holding the infinite
Space in our heart.

Here we can feel
Here we become
The ground
Of the waterfall.

Our water
Falls soft
And fast
And deep.

Our water
Shares creation
With all
That is created.

As we stand
In our peace
We give our water
Its form.

We form
Our path home
And the path
For those to follow.

We form
A love
That shines bright
For ever.

The love
We share
Colors the world
With peace.

Those we touch
Inspire to love,
Can touch
And heal.

Those we love
Become love
And the path
That leads home.

We connect
All
And everything
In love.

Like a Foehn

I call you out
And let you go
With every breath
Breathing out
And breathing in
So slowly

In between
I find you
And all that creation
Offers us
In possibility
In love
In vision
In what is
Eternally ours

Then time
Sweeps me away
Like a foehn
Blowing down
The form of life
The life that binds us
To each other
To service
And back
To all

The spirit
Of the wind
Sings to us
Beckons us
To follow
Over the distance
Into forever
Into Usness

Love Can Quicken

You surround me
With your voice,
 your smile,
 your touch,
And my limits
Dissolve.

You greet me
With your wisdom,
your knowing,
your caring,
And my heart
Opens.

You reach for me
With passion,
And strength,
And purity,
And the universe
Moves
To make room
For us.

We wait
Gathering energy
And love,
And combined faith,
For our time
To create
Destiny.

In the waiting
Eternal moments
Come one
After another.

In the waiting
Possibility opens
To connection.

In the waiting
Precious time
Opens eternally
And all is shifted
In the ways
That only love
Can quicken.

Move On

What happens to me
In the second that it takes
To break my heart
For tears to flow
And words to leave?

How do I fall
So far, so fast
That my shaking body
Cannot recognize
The second before
When my heart was whole?

What provokes me
To the point
Of picking up the pieces
And recreating myself
From old to new
Sticking possibility
Into spaces where pieces
Have disappeared forever,
Lost to destiny,
Lost to love,
Lost to the vision
Of what can be?

The pivotal moments
When my heart opens
And my breath stops
And my soul reaches
Into life
to take control
And redirect
And realign
And reposition
Into change,
Can suddenly occur,
Unexpectedly shift
Everything that is me,
Everything that is,
Everything and nothing.

And I am left
To blink and sigh
And move on
Again.

I want to own it,
Understand it,
Anticipate it,
Find joy in it.
But I don't see it coming
As I remain,
Heart open,
Waiting for the clarity
That will remove the need
For tearful silence.

Of Angels

All I know of angels
I can see in your eyes.
The deep blue of heaven
Moves me like the sea.
Lifts me up with wings
Of unending possibility,
Into the depths of my soul.

Your love guides and protects me
Like a steadfast guardian,
Sentry at the threshold of my fear,
Banishing all potential harm
Allowing light and love to fill me,
Your golden glow surrounds me
Like a pocket of tender safety.

Your hands reach out to me
And reveal your sacred gift,
So simple and so elegant,
Merely all that I AM
And all that I can be,
Because you love me enough
To let your eyes lead the way.

And so my humble heart opens
And reaches for you in kind,
With an overwhelming desire
To move you completely,
To move you with me in tones,
In the rhythm that is ours
And ours alone.

Within that glorious rhythm
We connect to all creation,
Your angel wings enfold me,
Your gentle spirit infolds me,
And we become the divine creator
And all that is our good experience,
In truth, in love, in faith, through you.

Over and over

I see us
in the height
of our rapture,
Our soul clear
Our souls clear.

And in the clarity
A golden triangle
Of divine will
Aligned with our wills,
Divine love
that pours through us
with each motion
with each breath
mine into yours,
Divine action
that will allow us
to find our way
back
to eachother.

Our flame
holds us here,
our flame
burns bright
transforming our soul
transforming our souls
transforming creation
transforming us.

I love you so.

Sighs and Whispers

Remembering
Our most poignant sounds,
Our colors
And forms,
The tender touch
And heavenly smell
The delectable taste
Of our connection.

Remembering
These touchstones
Provides the starting point
To our journey
Through undiscovered
Dimensions
To all dimension
To simultaneous time
And NOTIME.

How is such depth
Possible
Between two souls
So brand new
To each other
In the present?

What button
Opened all doors
And propelled us,
Compelled us
To heaven
And back
So quickly?

Very early
We wondered
At the depth
Of our intimacy.
Now we wonder
At the endless

Possibility of intimacy
That constantly
Presents us
With more of US.

We share this all
With sighs and whispers,
With words and ideas,
With exchange
Of the senses,
With unified
Essence,
And boundless love.

I hold you here
With every breath.
I hold you where
Breath is
No longer needed.
I hold you
With arms
And eyes
And heart
And soul.
I hold you now
And always.

Slips Naturally

Sometimes
We can look around
And our world
Fits us perfectly
With hard work
Measures of success
Growing families
Homes of comfort.

And then we are drawn
Unexplainably
Into the known/unknown
With an inspiration,
Intuition
Or a whim.

If we can slip naturally
Into spirit
We are swept away
By eternity's movement
Within and without us,
Because and beside us.
It occurs in slow motion
We do not
Want it to end.
But it does.
And we are left
Changed.

In the change
We are left
To give texture,
Light and sensation
To what
We have become.

Left to translations
Of our own design.
Left to choose

To reinvent and move on,
Or return
To what was once comfortable,
But is now
Just a memory
Of comfort.

small

I call on you
In the darkness
And wait in silence
For your comfort

I call on angels
In the stillness
And hope they fill me
So that I can walk alone
Again

I go along
Wondering
What is real
And what illusion
Searching for
What I can hold
In my heart
And breathe into
My soul

I long
To find a way
To create
What brings joy
Connection
Direction
But today
Am left empty
And small.

tears this morning

Many tears this morning
for all the things we say
and all the things we cannot say.
Life goes on
breath does not stop
yet death incurs
pulse quickens
and slows
and goes on
through death
any way.

The Call

I stand ready
To embrace
The challenge.

I stand firm
In the truth
Of my soul.

I stand tall
As my heart
Races forward
At unimagined speeds,
Following spirit
Following the call.

I look upward
For a vision
Of my soul's longing.
I see possibility
So sublime
That is whisks
Me away.

I fill quickly
With emptiness
And wait for you,
Quietly wait,
And wonder
What is real
In the waiting.

The Sun

The space we share
So vast and brilliant
Lit by our flame
Brightened by our light
Opens to allow
Ideas to be recognized,
Possibility to flow
Like a river,
More created
As more is realized
On and on.

I love to arrive
At that place
With you
Where we create
Reality
With recognition,
Intuition
And inspiration.
Where we become
That truth we share
The instant
We understand,
Respect
And move
The energy
Between us.

I live
Here in your arms,
Resting in the sound
Of your voice,
Breathing your breath,
Sharing your heartbeat,

Folding perfectly
Into your curves,
Like engaging
And releasing
The sun.

Through You

Through the tears
I remember
The way your hands
Held me,
The way your eyes
Carried me back
When my spirit
Gave way,
The way your voice
Grabbed my heart
And carried my soul.

In the silence
I hear your song,
Sung with a rhythm
That compels me
To join you,
That allows me
To become you,
That clarifies
So I may follow,
That suggests
What is possible.

In the stillness
I wait for you,
For the warmth
Of your closeness,
For your breath
As my own,
For the reach
And reverse
Of polarity.

I wait for
The one step
In our dance
To begin again
And again.

In the wait
So we find
Our beat
Again,
And we move
Our energy again,
And we shed
Our pain
Again,
And the world
Can breathe
Again,
And creation
Is healed
Again.

With the emptiness
I remain
Surrounded by you,
Immersed within you,
Imbued with desire,
Soaked with essence,
Slowly, carefully
Filling the space
With the physical
Memory of you,
Dying and leaving
Only to become
What is possible
Through you.

Together

I reach for you
And your colors fill me
And comfort me
Like a soft, warm,
Well used blanket.
They are my colors too.

I call for you
And your silvery voice
Calls back
And carries me away,
Through time,
Through light,
Into being.

I wait for you
Until the moon takes notice
And mercifully delivers me
To that place
Where we have always been,
And all ways will be,
In one breath.

I sigh for you,
Releasing magic to the night
Invoking impulse for depth.
So you move to me
With quiet elegance
And brilliant confidence,
Your magnetic response.

You touch me so,
Within an instant
And for eternity,
Including all dimension,
Embracing the essential,
Containing all of me
With all of you,
Together.

Welcome Home

To welcome you home
With a smile
With open arms
With a twin flame
Roaring
In the hearth of my heart
Is an honor
And a Godsend
That I give with humility
And accept with surrender.

To hear the sound
Of your sweet voice
Once again
With tones so clear
And true
They harmonize
Everything
Within me
Is what I await
Within each pause
Between breaths.

To drink your words
Like life's
Essential water
And feel them
Roll in waves
Throughout me
Endlessly
Quenching
My expansive thirst
Is the pulse
Of my vitality
And light.

You were so missed
You are so loved
We are so blessed
And so...

What's real

I see you in a quiet place
Where touch and sound and light
Are shrouded from what's real
Yet are all that is real.

I wonder of the fate
Of this half experience
Shared across the distance
And hidden from the rest.

I know this is a fragile state
Set to shatter
At any possible moment
It is so willed.

I am unsure if our intentions
Can protect us from a change
That consumes the flame
And splits the path.

I hold you where
Possibility allows
Togetherness
All ways.
Israel.

Write and Rewrite

What can we do
As we look
Far ahead
To what can be
In this twin flame,
Sacred scenario?

Here we stand
Faced with choices.
We can clear our way
To eachother
And open the door
To unlimited
Possibility,
Or remain entrenched
Within our lives
As we currently live them.
Creating the twin flame story
Of Thorn Bird variety.

As the picture clarifies,
As the scene unfolds,
I give sadness
To the fact
That we cannot find
Our way clear,
And begin to plan
My flight path,
One that will
Guide me safely
Back to who I am,
Before the thorns
Present themselves.

If the story was mine
To write and rewrite
I would end it so differently.
So I will continue
To hold space
In my heart
For all the possible

Glorious endings
That can be.
I hold them there
With light and love
And everything
I am
And everything
I can be,
Including yours.

You step back

You step back
I approach
Into light
Into forever

You smile
I sigh
and echoes
create the waves
that undulate
into heart beats
each beat
connecting
a shared life

You step up
I rise
to meet your
sweet breath
of life
I breathe in
and find release

You lead
I follow
you wait
I catch up
And the rhythm
creates life
where all
is possible
and intent
becomes birth.

www.ingramcontent.com/pod-product-compliance
Lightning Source LLC
Chambersburg PA
CBHW031002090426
42737CB00008B/640